Published by: Cross Media Ltd.
66-67 Wells Street, London W1T 3QB, UK
Tel: 020-7436-1960   Fax: 020-7436-1930

Project Manager: Kazuhiro Marumo
Editor: Yoko Takechi
Designer: Misa Watanabe
Photographer: Naomi Igawa, Hiroshi Mitani, Akira Kawai, Naoko Morine
Chef: Miyoko Yoshimura (Akasha Cooking School)
Coordinator: Asahiko Goto. Thanks to: Anthony Nott, Mary Thompson

ISBN 1-897701-03-9
Printed in Japan

All about Miso

Miso - the healthy option!

Miso, fermented soya bean paste, originated in China but has changed over the years and gradually adapted to Japanese soil. It appears that a fermented food, similar to the Japanese miso that we know today, was first produced during the Jomon Period (6000? - 300 B.C) as there are records about it dating back to that time. The popular fourteenth century saying, 'a bowl of miso a day keeps the doctor away' is still in use today and miso continues to be an important part of the Japanese breakfast.

When Japan was an farming country, miso was made by hand. The flavour would vary according to the local climate, products, and preference of the particular family. These days, homemade miso is less common and miso is generally mass produced. However, most families are very particular about the flavour of the miso and it is quite common for a newly married couple to argue over the taste.

Benefits of Miso

Perfectly balanced food

It has been said there is no food which is as perfectly balanced nutritionally as miso. Through the fermenting process, a lot of vitamins and essential amino acids (which are not contained in fresh soya beans) are created. Its high Vitamin E content helps the human body fight the aging process. Its amino acids help rid the body of harmful toxins (such as nicotine and alcohol), reduce blood cholesterol and prevent high blood pressure. The enzymes, which come from koji (a fermenting agent) help digestion.

	MISO 100g	CHICKEN (breast, with skin) 100g
calories	186kcal / 778kJ	203kcal / 849kJ
protein	13.1g	20.6g
fat	5.5g	12.3g
-saturated	0.88g	3.37g
-mono-unsat'd	1.07g	5.6g
-poly-unsat'd	3.21g	1.91g
cholesterol	0	80mg
vitamin E	0.9mg	0.3mg
calcium	130mg	5mg

Anti-carcinogenic proporties

Miso's capacity to help preventing various cancer is noteworthy. It is especially shows its ability on liver, stomach and bowel cancers. In Japan there are data which say that men who do not have miso soup at all have 50% higher death rate from stomach cancer than those who have it every day.

Types of Miso

Ingredients and process

Miso is made from soy beans, and usually rice, or less commonly barley is added. The ingredients are steamed, then mixed with a starter and left to ferment for between 6 month and five years.

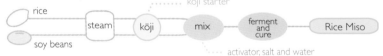

Varieties of Miso

The most common miso for home use is called Inaka-Miso, and is made from soy and rice. It can be roughly divided into 3 types by colour, red, white and intermediate. The difference in colour depends on

Red Miso   White Miso   Intermediate Miso

the ingredients and the length of fermenting time, a darker colour means the miso has been fermented longer and therefore has a stronger taste. There are also special types of miso from particular areas of Japan, which make use of local ingredients and climate.

How to make Japanese soup stock

One of the key ingredients in Japanese dishes is the soup stock:

Dashi - the basic Japanese soup stock

There are several types of popular dashi but the one made from kelp and bonito flakes is a good choice as it has a mild and smooth flavour and can be used in the same way as chicken stock in western cooking.
Learn this simple recipe and gradually increase your knowledge of Japanese food!

Makes 1 litre

1 sheet of drid kelp
(10cm x 10cm)
1 litre water
15g bonito flakes

1   Make a few slits in the kelp, and cook in water on a medium heat. Remove just before boiling.

2   Add the bonito flakes to the pan, bring to the boil, and strain.

*for vegetarians, use twice as much kelp and omit the bonito.

Other ingredients for dashi

Another popular ingredient for dashi is iriko (often called niboshi) - dried sardine. This is especially suitable for soup dishes (miso soup, noodle soup etc.). Dried shiitake mushrooms are also commonly used and dashi made from chicken, beef or pork are other good choices. Various kinds of instant dashi are also available in sachets, liquid and powdered form.

Instant dashi

Iriko

Shiitake

How to make shiitake dashi - perfect for vegetarians!

Makes 1 litre

5-6 dried shiitake mushrooms

1 litre water

Simply place the mushrooms in the water, leave for at least 1 hour, then strain. If you do not have time, boil once and leave for 10 minutes.

Miso Soup with Wakame and Tōfu

豆腐とわかめのみそ汁　*Tōfu to Wakame no Miso-shiru*

Serves 2

5g dried *wakame*

70g silken *tōfu*
(⅕ standard size block)

20g white miso

300 ml Japanese
soup stock

a handful of chives

* See page 6 how to make soup stock

1 Rinse the *wakame* and soak in water for 5 minutes. Cut into bite size pieces. Cut the *tōfu* into 1.5 cm cubes.

2 Heat the soup stock for 3-4 minutes and gently dissolve the miso in the soup.

3 Add the *wakame* and *tōfu* and heat gently for 5 minutes being careful not to let it boil. Garnish with chopped chives before serving.

Chunky Vegetable Miso Soup

● けんちん汁　Kenchin-jiru ●

Serves 2

1 small potato

¼ medium carrot

60g *konnyaku* (⅕ standard size block)

¼ leek

70g cotton *tōfu* (⅕ standard size block)

20g red miso

350 ml Japanese soup stock

½ tbsp sesame oil

* See page 6 how to make soup stock

1　Cut the *konnyaku*, peeled potato and carrot into very small pieces. Slice the leek diagonally, 2 cm in width.

2　Heat the sesame oil in a deep pan and stir-fry the *konnyaku* and vegetables. Add the soup stock and simmer until the ingredients have softened.

3　Crush the *tōfu* by hand and add to the pan. Gently dissolve the miso and remove from the heat before bringing it to the boil.

Simmered Mackerel with Miso Sauce

● サバのみそ煮 *Saba no Miso-ni* ●

This dish is popular with Japanese mums!
Enjoy its rich taste with white rice.

Serves 2

½ mackerel fillet
(one side of the body)

small piece
of fresh ginger
(for seasoning)

30g red miso

small piece
of fresh ginger
(for garnish)

some cooking foil

1 Cut the fish in half along the body, then cut two slits across each piece.

2 Boil [A] in a pan and add the mackerel (skin side up).

12

[A]
1 tsp thick soy sauce
3 tbsp *sake*
1 tbsp sugar
150 ml water

3

Slice the ginger thinly, sprinkle it over the mackerel and simmer for 5 minutes.

4 Ladle some soup from the pan into a small bowl. Mix in the miso and return it to the pan.

Tip!

By the time you cover the mackerel with foil it will have become very soft and delicate, so be sure to take care when shaking the pan.

5 Cover the mackerel with a piece of cooking foil slightly smaller than the pan in diameter.

6 Simmer for 12 minutes, occasionally shaking the pan so that the mackerel absorbs the sauce.

7 Serve the fish on a plate with the sauce. Garnish with grated ginger.

14

Grilled Aubergine with Miso Paste

● なすの田楽 *Nasu no Dengaku* ●

Serves 2

1 large aubergine

vegetable or
sunflower oil
for deep frying

½ egg yolk

sesame seeds
(for topping)

[A]

50g red miso

2 tbsp sugar

1 tbsp *sake*

1 tbsp *mirin*

1 Cut the aubergine in half lengthways. Heat the oil in a deep pan and fry both pieces, the skin side first, followed by the other side until they are soft. Drain well.

2 Put [A] into a small pan and simmer, stirring constantly. When it becomes sticky, remove from the heat and mix with the yolk.

3 Put the miso paste on the cut sides of the aubergine and grill until brown on top. Garnish with sesame seeds.

Konnyaku with Miso Dipping Sauce
こんにゃくの田楽　*Konnyaku no dengaku*

Serves 2

250g *konnyaku*
(1 standard size block)

400 ml Japanese
soup stock

[A- sesame-miso sauce]

20g red miso

1 tbsp sugar

1 tbsp *sake*

2 tbsp Japanese
soup stock

1 tbsp sesame paste
(or ground sesame)

[B- mustard-miso sauce]

30g white miso

1 tbsp sugar

1 tbsp *mirin*

1 tbsp *sake*

2 tbsp Japanese
soup stock

½ tsp Japanese mustard

* See page 6 how to make soup stock

1 Make some fine slits on the surface of the *konnyaku* with a knife, then cut it into 6 even pieces. Put the pieces in a pan of water, bring to a boil, then drain.

2 Make sauce [A]. Mix miso and sugar in a small pan, Add the *sake* and *mirin*, and put on a low heat, stirring constantly until it becomes glossy in appearance. Remove from the heat and add the sesame paste.

3 Make sauce [B] in the same way but use mustard instead of sesame paste. Put each piece of *konnyaku* on a skewer and serve with the dipping sauce.

Japanese Radish with Miso Sauce

● ふろふき大根 *Furofuki Daikon* ●

Serves 2

12 cm Japanese radish

10 cm × 10 cm
dried *konbu*

1 tsp soy sauce

[A]

50g red miso

40g sugar

1 tbsp *mirin*

1 egg yolk

1 Cut the radish into 3 cm slices. Make a cross shaped shallow slit on each side.

2 Put the *konbu* and radish in a pan with just enough water to cover them. Simmer until the radish is soft and add the soy sauce just before removing from the heat.

3 Put [A] into a saucepan and simmer while stirring until it thickens. Serve the radish with the sauce.

Miso Chicken Mince on Rice

● みそ味の鶏そぼろ *Miso-aji no Tori-soboro* ●

Serves 2

150g minced chicken

150 ml water

1 tsp grated ginger

2 tbsp red miso

2 tbsp *mirin*

1 tbsp *sake*

3 tbsp corn or potato flour mixed with same amount of water

2 portions of cooked rice

1 Put the chicken in a pan with the cold water, stir to loosen, then heat to a boil.

2 Lower the heat and add the *mirin*, miso and *sake* to the pan. When the chicken changes colour, add the corn flour (mixed with water) to thicken.

3 Serve the rice in a bowl with the chicken on top.

Pork Cutlet with Miso Sauce

● みそカツ Miso-katsu ●

Miso-katsu is a local speciality from the Nagoya area: Crispy cutlets and a sizzling miso sauce — a perfect combination!

Serves 2

2 pork loin chops
a pinch of salt
a pinch of pepper
a handful of plain flour
a handful of breadcrumbs
1 egg lightly beaten

1   Put [A] into a small sauce pan. Bring to the boil while stirring. Then lower the heat and simmer for 10 –15 minutes, stirring occasionally.

Miso-katsu

some vegetable oil for deep frying

50g cabbage

2 wedged slices of lemon

[A]

50 ml Japanese soup stock

70g red miso

30g white miso

1 tbsp *mirin*

2 tbsp *sake*

1 tbsp sugar

2 Make 4-5 cuts along each chop without cutting right through.

3 Season the chops with salt and pepper. Coat thinly in flour; dip into the beaten egg and coat with breadcrumbs.

4 Heat the oil in a deep frying pan. Deep fry pork until it floats on the surface of the oil.

5 Place the pork on kitchen paper to remove any excess oil. Cut into bite size pieces.

6

Shred the cabbage very thinly. Arrange on a plate with the cutlet.

7 Pour the miso sauce on top and serve with lemon.

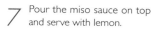

Green Salad with Miso Dressing

● 野菜サラダ みそドレッシング和え *Miso Doresshingu no Sarada* ●

Serves 2

5-6 lettuce leaves
12 cm cucumber
½ small onion
2 small tomatoes

[A]
2 tsp white miso
1 tbsp rice vinegar
2 tbsp vegetable oil

1 Tear the lettuce into bite size pieces and cut the cucumber and tomato into 1.5-2 cm cubes. Slice the onion into 2mm pieces, then put into a bowl of water for 10-15 minutes.

2 Put [A] into a small bowl and mix with a whisk to make the miso dressing sauce.

3 Put the vegetables into a salad bowl and serve with the sauce.

Wakame with Miso & Vinegar

わかめの酢みそ和え　*Wakame no Sumiso-ae*

* See page 6 how to make soup stock

Serves 2

5g dried *wakame*

1 spring onion

3 crabsticks

2 tbsp rice vinegar

[A]

1 tbsp red miso

2 tsp sugar

1 tsp Japanese soup stock

1. Soak the *wakame* in water for 5 minutes, drain and cut into bite size pieces. Cut the spring onion into 1.5 cm pieces and split the crabsticks into thin pieces.

2. Put [A] in a bowl and mix well. Then stir in the vinegar.

3. Put the *wakame* and onion in a sieve, pour boiling water through them, then mix the ingredients together with the sauce.

Miso flavoured stir-fried Vegetables

● 野菜のみそ炒め *Yasai no Miso-itame* ●

Serves 2

1 red pepper
1 green pepper
50g cabbage
½ carrot
1 tbsp white miso
2 tsp sugar
1 tsp *sake*
some vegetable oil for stir-frying

1 Cut the peppers, cabbage and carrot into bite size pieces.

2 Heat the oil in a frying pan and stir-fry the vegetables quickly on a high heat.

3 Slightly lower the heat and add the miso, sugar and *sake*. Stir and remove from the heat.

Simmered Pork and Vegetables with Miso

● 豚肉と野菜のみそ煮込み　*Butaniku to Yasai no Miso-nikomi* ●

* See page 6 how to make soup stock

Serves 2

100g blocked or thinly sliced pork

150g tinned bamboo shoots (boiled)

½ small onion

50g mange tout

150 ml Japanese soup stock

1 tbsp sugar

1 tbsp *sake*

30g white miso

1-2 tsp soy sauce

some vegetable oil for stir-frying

1 Cut the pork into bite size pieces, slice the onion into 2-3 mm pieces and stir-fry in a frying pan with some oil.

2 Add soup stock, sugar and *sake* and simmer for 5 minutes. Melt the miso into it and add the trimmed mange tout.

3 Simmer until the ingredients have absorbed the water, stirring occasionally. Add soy sauce just before removing from the heat.

34

Oyster Hot Pot with Miso

● かき鍋　*Kaki-Nabe* ●

Traditional 'cook-at-the-table' winter hot pot, which can also be cooked on a regular cooker.

Serves 4

400g oysters
(without shells)

1 leek

350g cotton *tōfu*
(1 standard size block)

100g *enoki* musrooms

100g *shimeji*
mushrooms

* See page 6 how to make soup stock

1   Rub the oysters with salt to remove the dirt and sand, then rinse and drain well.

[A]

800 ml Japanese
soup stock

100g red miso

100g white miso

5 tbsp sugar

100 ml *sake*

2 Slice the leek diagonally, 2 cm in width. Cut the *tōfu* into 8 even pieces. De-stem the *enoki* and *shimeji* mushrooms and break them into pieces.

3 Mix [A] well in a bowl. Put in a pan and bring to the boil.

4 Lower the heat, add the leek, oyster, mushrooms and finally the *tōfu*.

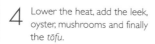

5 Once the ingredients are cooked, remove the pan from the heat.

6 Place the pan immediately on the table and serve onto individual plate.

Rice Porridge with Miso

みそ雑炊　Miso-Zōsui

Serves 2

300g cooked rice

400ml Japanese Soup Stock

2 tbsp red miso

½ leek

2 *shiitake* mushrooms

2 eggs, lightly beaten

* See page 6 how to make soup stock

1 Place the rice in a sieve, and rinse lightly in cold water, then drain well. De-stem the mushrooms and cut into 3 mm pieces. Slice the leek diagonally, into 1cm pieces.

2 Boil the soup stock in a pan. Dissolve the miso into it and add the leek and mushrooms. Simmer for 3 minutes. Add the rice and bring to a boil again.

3 Just before removing the pan from the heat, add the eggs and stir quickly.

40

Grilled Rice Ball

● 焼きおにぎり *Yaki-onigiri* ●

Makes 2 balls

200g cooked rice
2 tsp red miso
I tsp sugar
some *nori* or *shiso* leaves (optional)

1 Wet the palms of your hands. Take half the rice and make it into a triangular shape. Make another 'ball' with the remaining rice.

2 Mix the miso with the sugar. Spread it on the surface of the rice balls and grill both sides until browned.

3 Wrap in *nori* or *shiso* leaves.

Miso Biscuits

みそクッキー   *Miso kukkī*   ●

An ideal way to enjoy the delicate sweetness of miso!

Makes 20 biscuits

200g plain flour

1 small egg,
lightly beaten

100g butter

80g sugar

20g white miso

20g sliced almonds
(optional)

1. Put the butter in a bowl and soften with a spatula. Mix with the sugar and miso.

2 Add the beaten egg gradually,
   then the flour (sieved), and
   almonds. Mix well but gently.

3

Place the dough on a sheet
of cling film. Roll it into a
pole shape, 5 cm in diameter.
Put in the fridge for at least
30 minutes.

Miso kukkī

4   Pre-heat the oven to 180°C. Take the dough out of the fridge and cut into 5mm slices.

5

Put the slices on a greased baking tray and bake for about 20 minutes until slightly browned.

• Guide to ingredients - Miso •

Daikon	——	Japanese radish
Dashi	——	Japanese soup stock
Enoki	——	very thin white mushrooms
Katsuobushi	——	bonito flakes
Komezu	——	rice vinegar
Konbu	——	kelp
Konnyaku	——	vegetarian jelly made from devil's tongue plant (Japanese mountain vegetable)
Mirin	——	cooking sake (sweet)
Niboshi	——	dried sardine
Nori	——	sheet of dried seaweed
Sake	——	Japanese rice wine
Shiitake	——	variety of mushroom
Shimeji	——	small brown-topped mushrooms
Shōyu	——	soy sauce
Shiso	——	beefsteak plant
Tōfu	——	bean curd
Wakame	——	variety of seaweed